vemytotebag

THIS IS NOT
louis vuitton
not hermes
NOT a billy
jeromeDREYFUSS
EVEN NOT,
monop'

#il

TOTE BAGS

20 CREATIVE PROJECTS

SONIA LUCANO

Photographs: Frédéric Lucano
Stylist: Sonia Lucano

INTRODUCTION

Simple cotton tote bags first became popular as a sustainable alternative to plastic shopping bags. Soon they were being used by brands for advertising purposes, and now totes can be seen everywhere, out on the street, in a huge range of different styles. The tote bag is the ultimate fashion statement and can be adapted for any occasion.

This book includes straightforward instructions for making a basic tote bag, along with twenty ideas for personalizing it to suit your own tastes. If you'd prefer to avoid the sewing part, it's easy to find plain tote bags in craft shops and wholefood stores. Then all you have to do is add a personal touch!

A range of different techniques are used to customize the basic bag, including embroidery, painting, dyeing, transfers, quilting, stamping and more. Each project is marked with its level of difficulty, but rest assured that all of them are within the reach of enthusiastic beginners. So dive in!

CONTENTS

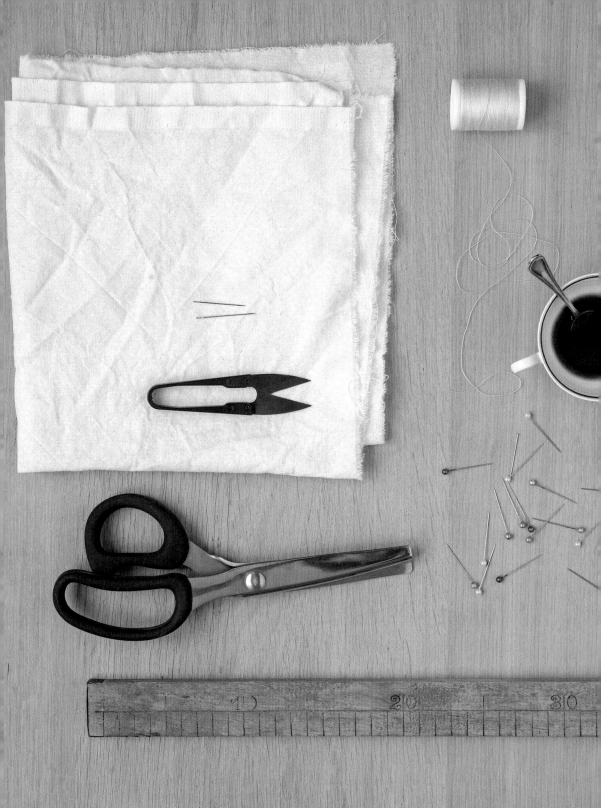

MAKE A BASIC TOTE BAG

Level of difficulty
Easy

Time required
1½ hrs

Materials
1 piece of unbleached
   cotton, measuring
   100 × 150 cm
Unbleached cotton thread
Iron

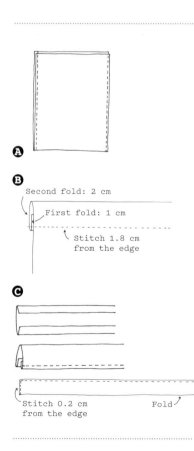

A

B

Second fold: 2 cm

First fold: 1 cm

Stitch 1.8 cm
from the edge

C

Stitch 0.2 cm   Fold
from the edge

1. First wash the cotton. This
step is essential, firstly because
unbleached cotton shrinks when washed,
and secondly because it looks more
attractive when slightly crumpled.

2. Iron the cotton, then cut out a
rectangle measuring 86 × 39 cm (for the
bag) and two strips measuring 65 × 7 cm
(for the handles). These measurements
allow for a 1-cm seam along the sides
of the bag and a 3-cm hem at the top.

3. Oversew the two long sides of the
cotton rectangle to prevent it from
fraying. Then fold it in half and
stitch the oversewn sides 1 cm from
the edge, right up to the top of the
bag, as shown in diagram **A**. Iron.

4. Fold over 1 cm at the top edge of the
bag, then fold it over again by 2 cm,
tucking the first fold underneath,
as shown in diagram **B**. Use the iron to
press this hem flat. Now stitch all the
way round the top, 1.8 cm from the edge.

5. To make the handles, use the iron
to press a 1-cm fold along each side
of the handle strips. Fold each handle
lengthwise, then press again, as shown
in diagram **C**.

6. Stitch around the three sides of
the handles, 0.2 cm from the edge.

7. Pin the handles on both sides of
the bag, 7 cm from the edge, leaving
a length of 3 cm to hang inside the
bag. Stitch on the handles by sewing
a rectangle measuring 2 × 1.5 cm to
fix each end in place.

TECHNIQUES FOR CUSTOMIZING YOUR TOTE

Here is a sample of the many different techniques that can be used to personalize a tote bag.

Transfer: An easy technique with fast results. Scan the motif you want to use and print it onto transfer paper. Place the transfer face down on the tote and press with a hot iron. Leave to cool, then gently peel off the protective backing.

Embroidery: A range of different stitches can be used to create varied effects, including chain stitch, running stitch, back stitch, detached chain or satin stitch. See page 64 for some basic examples.

Fabric painting: Use fabric paint to reproduce your chosen design. Leave to dry, then carefully iron the reverse side of the fabric to fix the colour.

French quilting: Draw your design on a double layer of cotton and sew over the outlines in running stitch (see page 64), joining the two layers together but leaving an opening at one end. Then create volume by filling the space between the layers with thick cotton yarn, pulled into place with a blunt tapestry needle.

Tie-dye: Twist the fabric to make a knot in the centre. Heat water containing salt and dye in a large bowl. Lower the fabric into the liquid, just covering the knot, and leave it to soak, following the instructions on the packet. Rinse with cold water and undo the knot. Leave to dry and then iron the fabric.

Stamping: Carve a motif out of a potato to create a simple stamp. Pour fabric paint onto a paper plate and soak the potato in it. Stamp the motif as required. Iron the fabric on the reverse side to fix the image.

CUSTOMIZED TOTE BAGS

'THIS IS NOT' TOTE

Level of difficulty
Easy

Time required
30 mins

Technique
Transfer

Materials
1 basic tote bag
Inkjet transfer paper
Iron

This style of bag is simple to make since the transfer method does not require any special skills. You can also use a PC to create your own typographical motifs.

Instructions

1. Scan the design on page 65 and enlarge it to fit the size of your bag. Print it on a sheet of transfer paper.

2. Cut off any extra margin around the letters and place the design face down in the centre of the bag, then press with a hot iron. Be sure to follow the instructions on the transfer paper packaging: don't use the steam function on the iron (the transfer won't stick properly), and keep the iron moving, to avoid burning the fabric.

3. Leave the transfer to cool and then gently peel off the protective backing.

Tip

Always iron a transfer on the reverse side. Ironing the right side is a sure way to ruin your design!

STRIPED TOTE

Level of difficulty
Easy

Time required
30 mins

Technique
Embroidery

Materials
1 basic tote bag
Dressmaking pencil or
    tailor's chalk
Ruler
1 skein of gold
    embroidery thread

This golden running stitch is very
simple to do but the results look
striking and elegant.

Instructions

1. Starting 2 cm from the top edge
of the bag, draw ten lines across the
centre of the bag, each 31 cm long and
spaced 3 cm apart.

2. Separate a double strand of gold
thread from the skein. Cut into 40 cm
lengths.

3. Use running stitch (see page 64)
to embroider along the lines.

POCKET TOTE

Level of difficulty
Medium

Time required
1 hr

Technique
Stitching

Materials
1 basic tote bag
1 square of printed
   fabric, 26 × 26 cm
1 pearlized button,
   1.5 cm across
1 piece of leather or
   cotton braid measuring
   10 × 0.5 cm

**The colourful pocket on this bag
gives it a vintage look.**

Instructions

1. Oversew around the edges of the
square of printed fabric.

2. To create tucks on the bottom
corners of the pocket, fold the square
of fabric in two diagonally, right
sides together, and then pin in place.
Stitch across the bottom corner at a
right angle, as shown in diagram **A**.
Unfold the square and repeat the
process on the other bottom corner.

3. Use an iron to press a 2-cm hem along
the top edge of the pocket. Stitch
along this fold, 1.8 cm from the edge,
as shown in diagram **B**.

4. Press a 1-cm fold along the other
three sides of the pocket.

5. Pin the pocket onto the centre of
the bag and oversew it by hand along
the lower three sides, using small
stitches, as shown in diagram **C**.

6. Sew the button onto the top hem of
the pocket, in the centre.

7. Fold the piece of braid in two to
form a loop for the button, then sew
the ends onto the bag, about 3 cm
above the button.

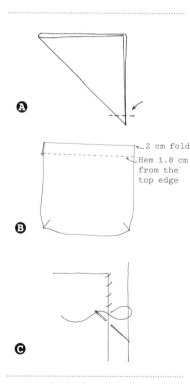

A

2 cm fold
Hem 1.8 cm
from the
top edge

B

C

BIRD AND BRANCH TOTE

Level of difficulty
Medium

Time required
1 hr

Technique
Fabric painting

Materials
1 basic tote bag
Tracing paper
Dressmaker's carbon
   paper
Iron
Pencil
Black fabric paint
Orange fabric paint
Fine paintbrush

This stylish silhouette is painted carefully with a fine brush.

Instructions

1. Trace the silhouette of the branch from page 66 and enlarge it with a photocopier to fit the size of your bag. Use the carbon paper to transfer the outline directly onto the bag.

2. Paint the branch with the black fabric paint, using a fine brush.

3. Leave to dry and then carefully iron the bag on the reverse side to fix the image.

4. If you wish, you can now add one or more birds to the branches. Trace the bird motif from page 66 and enlarge it with a photocopier to the size you want. Use the carbon paper to copy the outline directly onto the bag, then paint the bird with orange paint.

Tip

If you don't have dressmaker's carbon paper, place the photocopied motif inside the bag so that it shows through, and paint over it.

'BE HAPPY OR DIE' TOTE

Level of difficulty
Medium

Time required
2 hrs

Technique
Embroidery

Materials
1 basic tote bag
Tracing paper
Dressmaker's carbon
    paper
Pencil
1 skein of red embroidery
    thread

A head-turning motif to help you remember that it's a wonderful life!

Instructions

1. Trace the design on page 66 and enlarge it with a photocopier to fit the size of your bag. Use the carbon paper to copy the outline directly onto the bag.

2. Separate a double strand of red thread from the skein. Cut to a length of 50 cm.

3. Embroider the words 'be happy' and 'DIE' in chain stitch. Embroider the word 'OR' in straight stitch (see page 64).

Tip

If you don't have any dressmaker's carbon paper, place the photocopied motif inside the bag so that it shows through, and draw over it.

DOUBLE TOTE

Level of difficulty
Medium
Time required
2½ hrs
Technique
Sewing
Materials
1 piece of fabric with a
    star print, 50 × 100 cm
1 piece of polka-dot
    fabric, 50 × 100 cm
Thread to match both
    fabrics
1 skein of neon yellow
    embroidery thread
1 grey pearlized button

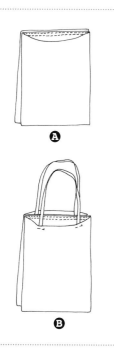

This double bag offers lots of options.
You can use the same fabric in two
contrasting colours or prints, or
even try using two different fabrics.

Instructions

1. Cut out one bag from the star-print
fabric and another from the polka-
dot fabric, following the basic tote
bag pattern on page 7. Cut out the two
handles from the polka-dot fabric.

2. Make the two bags, again following
the instructions on page 7. Assemble
the handles but don't attach them yet.

3. Pin the bags together along the
top edge and then sew two lines of
stitching, one 0.2 cm below the edge
to hold both bags together, and another
below it, over the hems of both bags,
as shown in diagram **A**.

4. Pin the handles onto the two
outer sides of the bag, as shown in
diagram **B**. Stitch a rectangle at each
end to fix the handles in place.

5. Use a double strand of embroidery
thread to sew the button onto the
inside rear face of the bag, in the
upper centre. Create two buttonholes
in the central and front panels, in
front of the button: do this by cutting
a horizontal slit, overstitching its
edge, then saddle-stitching around it.

6. Embroider three little crosses in
the bottom left corner of the starry
fabric, using two strands of yellow
embroidery thread.

FRINGED TOTE

Level of difficulty
Easy

Time required
1 hr

Technique
Sewing

Materials
1 basic tote bag
Iron
Ruler
Dressmaking pencil
Craft knife with new blade
1 strip of unbleached
    cotton, 76 × 12 cm
1 strip of iron-on
    interfacing, 76 × 12 cm

Add a fringe to your tote bag for a boho look.

Instructions

1. Place the interfacing on top of the strip of cotton. Iron to bond both layers together, according to the manufacturer's instructions.

2. Draw a series of 10-cm lines across the width of the strip with a dressmaking pencil, 1 cm apart.

3. Leaving a 2-cm uncut space at one side, cut down the lines with the craft knife, creating a fringe. Be sure not to cut across the entire width of the strip.

4. Pin the strip at the top of the bag with the fringe hanging down. Allow the ends of the strip to overlap by 1 cm, and fit the strip neatly around the edge, as shown in diagram **A**.

5. Sew two lines of stitching around the top of the bag, first 0.2 cm from the edge and then 1.5 cm from the edge, as shown in diagram **B**.

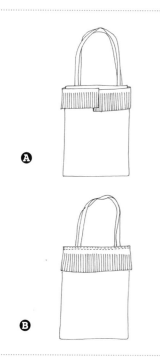

A

B

CLOUD MINI-TOTE

Level of difficulty
Difficult

Time required
3 hrs

Technique
Sewing + French quilting

Materials
1 piece of unbleached
    cotton, 100 × 150 cm
Unbleached cotton thread
Iron
Tracing paper
Dressmaker's carbon paper
Pencil
Thick cotton yarn,
    in white or cream
1 blunt tapestry needle

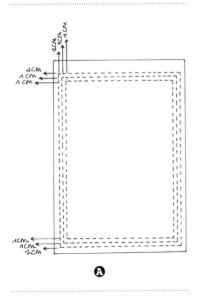

A

This small bag is adorned with a cloud and raindrops made using a technique called French quilting or *boutis*.

Instructions

1. First wash the cotton. This step is essential, firstly because unbleached cotton shrinks when washed, and secondly because it looks more attractive when slightly crumpled.

2. Iron the fabric, then cut out one rectangle measuring 86 × 39 cm and another measuring 43 × 33 cm (for the main body of the bag), plus two strips measuring 60 × 6 cm (for the handles). An allowance for the side seams (1 cm) and the hem at the top of the bag (3 cm) is included in these measurements.

3. Oversew the long edges of both cotton rectangles.

4. Pin the smaller of the two rectangles over the reverse side of the larger one, making sure it is positioned centrally at one end. Trace the motifs of the cloud and raindrops from page 67 and enlarge them to the size you want, using a photocopier if necessary. Use the carbon paper and pencil to copy them onto the double layer of cotton, on its right side.

5. Use a running stitch to sew around the outlines of the motifs and along their inner lines. Then sew three lines around the edges of the double rectangle, as shown in diagram **A**.

CLOUD MINI-TOTE
(continued)

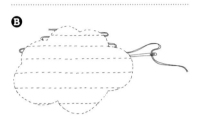

6. Turn the fabric reverse side up. Thread the tapestry needle with the thick cotton yarn. Push the needle into the fabric at the edge of one of the stitched motifs. Pass it between the layers of fabric, and pull it out at the other side, leaving a raised line of yarn between the layers. Continue to fill the motif in this way, as shown in diagram **B**. This will create a quilted effect. Do the same for all the motifs.

7. Fold the large rectangle in half, right side to right side. Stitch along the oversewn sides, 1 cm from the edge, to form the body of the bag.

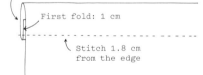

Second fold: 2 cm

First fold: 1 cm

Stitch 1.8 cm
from the edge

8. Make a 1-cm fold around the top edge of the bag, then tuck it under to make a 2-cm fold, as shown in diagram **C**. Iron the hem to flatten it, then stitch it down, 1.8 cm from the edge.

9. To make the handles, use the iron to press a 1-cm fold along each side of the handle strips. Fold each handle lengthwise, then press again, as shown in diagram **D**.

10. Stitch around the three sides of the handles, 0.2 cm from the edge.

11. Pin the handles on both sides of the bag, 5 cm from the edge, leaving a length of 3 cm to hang inside the bag. Stitch them in place along the hem.

Stitch 0.2 cm
from the edge   Fold

TIE-DYE TOTE

Level of difficulty
Easy

Time required
1 hr

Technique
Dyeing

Materials
1 basic tote bag
Coarse salt
Green fabric dye
    (for hand use)
Iron
1 matching grosgrain
    ribbon, 120 × 2 cm

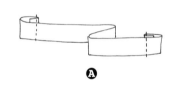

A

This project may seem tricky but there's no need to worry. The beauty of tie-dye is that even imperfect results still look good.

Instructions

1. Twist the bag lengthwise and then tie a tight knot in its centre.

2. Heat water in a large bowl and then add the coarse salt and the dye (follow the instructions on the dye packaging). Lower the bottom of the bag into the liquid until the knot is partially covered. Leave it to soak for at least half an hour, stirring the dye from time to time. Make sure the dye does not splash onto the top of the bag or the handles.

3. Rinse the bag with cold water and then undo the knot. Leave the bag to dry and then iron it.

4. Cut the ribbon into two equal pieces. Make a 0.5-cm fold on each end and then a second fold of 1 cm, as shown in diagram **A**. Iron to flatten, then stitch the ends 0.8 cm from the edge of the ribbon.

5. Pin one length of ribbon to each side of the bag, 10 cm from the top in a centred position. Sew them in place by sewing a 1.5 × 1 cm rectangle in back stitch at the end of each one. Then tie the ribbons in a bow.

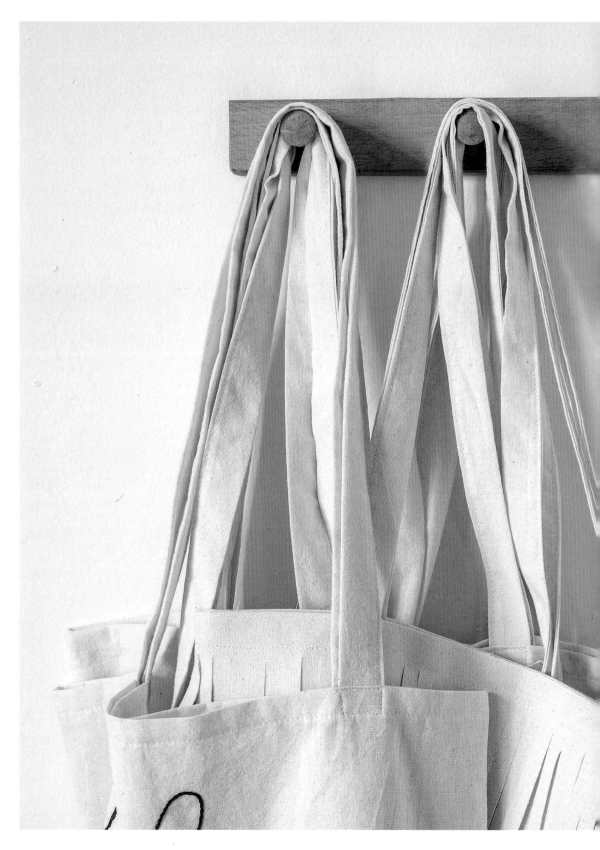

LIBERTY-PRINT TOTE

Level of difficulty
Medium

Time required
1 hr

Technique
Sewing + fabric painting

Materials
1 basic tote bag
1 square piece of
   Liberty-print cotton
   fabric, 30 × 30 cm
Green fabric paint
Fine paintbrush
Dressmaker's carbon paper
Pencil
Iron

The floral print gives this bag a traditional touch but the overpainted figures add a modern edge.

Instructions

1. Slightly fray the edges of the Liberty fabric by teasing out the strands of thread with a pin.

2. Trace the number of your choice from page 67. Enlarge it with a photocopier and use the carbon paper to transfer it onto the bottom right corner of the fabric.

3. Use the fine brush to paint on the figures, then iron the fabric on the reverse side to fix the colour.

4. Pin the fabric to the centre of the bag, then stitch it all the way round, 1 cm from the edge.

Tip

If you don't have any dressmaker's carbon paper, place the photocopied motif inside the bag so that it shows through, and paint over it.

SEQUINNED TOTE

Level of difficulty
Medium

Time required
1 hr

Technique
Embroidery

Materials
1 basic tote bag
Pink sequins
Matching cotton thread

A scattering of pink sequins contrasts with the natural colour of an unbleached cotton tote bag.

Instructions

Sew the sequins at random on the front of the bag. Make sure to add a few to the lower part of the handles.

TASSELLED TOTE

Level of difficulty
Medium

Time required
3 hrs (includes making
  the bag)

Technique
Sewing

Materials
1 piece of unbleached
  cotton, measuring
  100 × 150 cm
1 piece of Liberty-
  print cotton fabric,
  20 × 40 cm
Iron
1 piece of soft leather
  in navy blue, 12 ×
  12 cm
1 waxed cotton shoelace
  in navy blue
Fabric glue
Craft knife with new
  blade
2 clothes pegs

**A more traditional style of bag,
with reinforced corners and removable
leather tassels.**

Instructions

1. First wash the cotton. This
step is essential, firstly because
unbleached cotton shrinks when washed,
and secondly because it looks more
attractive when slightly crumpled.

2. Iron the cotton, then cut out two
rectangles measuring 43 × 39 cm (for
the bag) and two strips measuring
65 × 7 cm (for the handles). An
allowance for the side seams (1 cm)
and the hem at the top of the bag (3 cm)
is included in these measurements.

3. Oversew the two long sides of the
two rectangles.

4. Cut the Liberty fabric into four
triangles of equal size. Fold a hem of
0.5 cm along the long side of each one
and then press it with an iron. Pin a
triangle over a lower corner of one of
the large rectangles, and stitch it
0.2 cm from the inside edge, as shown
in diagram **Ⓐ**. Repeat this process
with the other three corners of the
bag (two triangles on the front, two
on the back).

5. Place the two large rectangles on
top of each other, with right sides
facing. Join them to form the body of
the bag by stitching along the three
lower sides, 1 cm from the edge.

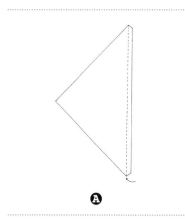

Ⓐ

TASSELLED TOTE

(continued)

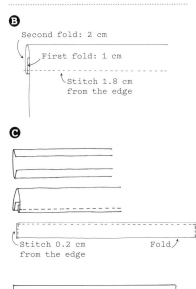

B

Second fold: 2 cm

First fold: 1 cm

Stitch 1.8 cm
from the edge

C

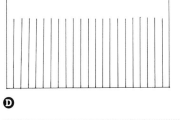

Stitch 0.2 cm   Fold
from the edge

D

6. Fold over 1 cm at the top edge of the bag, then fold it over again by 2 cm, tucking the first fold underneath, as shown in diagram **B**. Use the iron to press this hem flat. Now stitch all the way round the top, 1.8 cm from the edge.

7. To make the handles, use the iron to press a 1-cm fold along each side of the handle strips. Fold each handle lengthwise, then press again, as shown in diagram **C**.

8. Stitch around the three sides of the handles, 0.2 cm from the edge.

9. Pin the handles on both sides of the bag, 7 cm from the edge, leaving a length of 3 cm to hang inside the bag. Stitch on the handles by sewing a rectangle measuring 2 × 1.5 cm to fix each end in place.

10. Make the tassels: use the craft knife to cut the piece of leather into two identical strips, each measuring 12 × 6 cm. Create a fringe by making 4.5-cm cuts across the width of the strips, 0.5 cm apart, as shown in diagram **D**.

11. Put glue along the part of the leather with no cuts. Position the end of the shoelace across the glued strip and roll the rectangle in on itself, making sure that the lace is held firmly. Hold the tassel together with a clothes peg while the glue dries. Repeat this process with the other tassel, gluing it to the other end of the shoelace. Tie the finished lace loosely around one handle of the bag.

GEOMETRIC TOTE

Level of difficulty
Easy

Time required
1½ hrs

Technique
Stamping

Materials
1 basic tote bag
1 potato
Kitchen paper
Craft knife with new
  blade
Neon fabric paint in the
  colour of your choice
Paper plate
Iron

This tote bag with printed geometric motifs has a Scandinavian feel.

Instructions

1. Cut the potato in half and carve one side into the shape of a triangle, 1 cm high. Dry your potato stamp with kitchen paper to remove any starch.

2. Pour the fabric paint onto a paper plate and dip the stamp in it. Check the motif first by printing onto a sheet of paper.

3. Stamp on the triangles one by one, in horizontal lines.

4. Let the paint dry, then iron the fabric on the reverse side to fix the colour.

Tip

To add variety to your design, leave empty spaces here and there between the triangles.

NUMBERED TOTE

Level of difficulty
Easy

Time required
1 hr

Technique
Fabric painting

Materials
1 basic tote bag
Tracing paper
Pencil
Dressmaker's carbon paper
Green fabric paint
Fine paintbrush
1 pearlized button

Everybody has a lucky number, so why not add yours to this bag?

Instructions

1. Trace the number of your choice from page 68, then enlarge it with a photocopier to the size you want. Use the carbon paper to transfer the outline directly onto the bag.

2. Paint the number with the green fabric paint, using a fine paintbrush.

3. Leave to dry and then carefully iron the bag on the reverse side to fix the image.

4. Sew the button onto the inside of the bag's back, in the middle of the top edge. Create a buttonhole on the front of the bag, to line up with the button: do this by cutting a horizontal slit, overstitching its edge, then saddle-stitching around it.

Tip

If you don't have any dressmaker's carbon paper, place the photocopied motif inside the bag so that it shows through, and paint over it.

DEATH VALLEY TOTE

Level of difficulty
Easy

Time required
30 mins

Technique
Transfer

Materials
1 basic tote bag
Inkjet transfer paper
Iron

A bag with a touch of the Wild West.

Instructions

1. Scan the design on page 69 and enlarge it to fit the size of your bag. Print it on a sheet of transfer paper.

2. Cut off any extra paper around the motif and place the design face down in the centre of the bag, then press with a hot iron. Be sure to follow the instructions on the transfer paper packaging: don't use the steam function on the iron (the transfer won't stick properly), and keep the iron moving, to avoid burning the fabric.

3. Leave the transfer to cool and then gently peel off the protective backing.

Tip

Always iron a transfer on the reverse side. Ironing the right side is a sure way to ruin your design!

FAIRYTALE TOTE WITH ZIP

Level of difficulty
Difficult

Time required
3 hrs (includes making
the bag)

Technique
Appliqué + embroidery

Materials
1 piece of unbleached
cotton, 100 × 150 cm
in size
Unbleached cotton thread
Iron
1 beige invisible zip,
40 cm long
1 brown bias binding,
50 × 2.5 cm
1 skein of yellow
embroidery yarn
1 leather thong or cotton
shoelace, 60 × 0.5 cm
Tracing paper
Pencil
Dressmaker's carbon paper

A tote bag fit for a princess!

Instructions

1. First wash the cotton. This
step is essential, firstly because
unbleached cotton shrinks when washed,
and secondly because it looks more
attractive when slightly crumpled.

2. Iron the cotton, then cut out two
rectangles measuring 82 × 39 cm (for
the bag) and two strips measuring
65 × 7 cm (for the handles). An
allowance for the side seams (1 cm)
and the hem at the top of the bag (3 cm)
is included in these measurements.

3. To make the handles, use the iron
to press a 1-cm fold along each side
of the handle strips. Fold each handle
lengthwise, then press again, as shown
in diagram **Ⓐ**.

4. Stitch around the three sides of
the handles, 0.2 cm from the edge.

Ⓐ

Stitch 0.2 cm   Fold
from the edge

51

FAIRYTALE TOTE WITH ZIP

(continued)

5. Oversew all four sides of the rectangle. Fold it in half, right sides facing, and sew down both sides, 1 cm from the edge. Turn the bag right side out and iron.

6. Pin the handles on both sides of the bag, 7 cm from the edge, leaving a length of 3 cm to hang inside the bag. Pin the open zip, right side up, along one of the folds at the top of the bag. Repeat this process with the other half of the zip on the other side. Sew in the zip lengthwise, 1 cm from the edge. Iron.

7. Continue with the appliqué: unfold the strip of bias binding and iron it to form a curve. Mark the centre of the binding and line it up with the centre of the bag. Pin it in position, forming the shape of a banner (see page 69). Fix it in place by oversewing around its edges with unbleached cotton thread.

8. Trace the phrase 'once upon a time' from page 69 and use a photocopier to enlarge it to the size you want. Use carbon paper to transfer it onto the bias binding. Take a double strand of yellow embroidery yarn from the skein and embroider the letters in chain stitch (see page 64).

9. Thread the thong or shoelace through the slider of the zip and tie it in a knot.

EYE TEST TOTE

Level of difficulty
Easy

Time required
30 mins

Technique
Transfer

Materials
1 basic tote bag
Inkjet transfer paper
Iron

This bag features rows of letters in graduating sizes, as seen on an optician's chart.

Instructions

1. Scan the design on page 70 and enlarge it to fit the size of your bag. Print it on a sheet of transfer paper.

2. Cut off any extra paper around the motif and place the design face down in the centre of the bag, then press with a hot iron. Be sure to follow the instructions on the transfer paper packaging: don't use the steam function on the iron (the transfer won't stick properly), and keep the iron moving, to avoid burning the fabric.

3. Leave the transfer to cool and then gently peel off the protective backing.

Tip

Always iron a transfer on the reverse side. Ironing the right side is a sure way to ruin your design!

SKULL TOTE

Level of difficulty
Medium

Time required
6 hrs

Technique
Embroidery

Materials
1 basic tote bag
Tracing paper
Pencil
Dressmaker's carbon
    paper
1 skein of black
    embroidery yarn

The black embroidery and floral designs make this skull motif very striking.

Instructions

1. Trace the design on page 71, then enlarge it with a photocopier to the size you want. Use the carbon paper to copy it directly onto the bag.

2. Embroider over the lines with a double strand of black yarn, using chain stitch, running stitch and detached chain stitch (see page 64). The diagram on page 71 will show you which stitches go where.

Tip

If you don't have any dressmaker's carbon paper, place the photocopied motif inside the bag so that it shows through, and draw over it.

#ILOVEMYTOTEBAG

Level of difficulty
Medium

Time required
3 hrs

Technique
Embroidery

Materials
1 basic tote bag
1 strip of dark brown
   leather, 130 × 2.5 cm
Craft knife
Rotary punch
Bradawl
Unbleached heavy-duty
   thread
1 skein of deep red
   embroidery yarn
Dressmaker's carbon paper
Tracing paper
Pencil

A thoroughly modern tote bag with stylish leather handles.

Instructions

1. Cut the strip of leather in half to obtain two strips of equal length.

2. Use the rotary punch to mark out a square measuring 1.7 × 1.7 cm at the ends of each handle. Enlarge the holes with the bradawl.

3. Position the handles on the top edge of the bag, 7 cm from the sides. Use saddle stitch (see page 64) to sew them in place with the heavy-duty thread.

4. Trace the hashtag motif from page 70. Enlarge it with a photocopier to the size you need and use dressmaker's carbon paper to copy it onto the front of the bag, 8 cm from the bottom. Embroider the words in chain stitch (see page 64), using a double strand of red embroidery yarn.

Tips

Instead of using a rotary punch, you could simply make holes at regular intervals with the bradawl.

If you don't have any dressmaker's carbon paper, place the photocopied motif inside the bag so that it shows through, and draw over it.

LEATHER TOTE

Level of difficulty
Medium

Time required
3 hrs

Technique
Sewing

Materials
1 piece of tanned leather
Orange heavy-duty thread
Contact glue
Rotary punch
Bradawl
Craft knife with new
   blade
Clothes pegs

This plain leather bag looks simple but has an elegance all its own.

Instructions

1. Using the craft knife, cut out two leather rectangles measuring 37 × 40 cm and four strips measuring 65 × 2 cm.

2. Arrange the leather rectangles with wrong sides facing. Glue a 0.5 cm seam along the two sides and the bottom of the bag.

3. Run the rotary punch along the three glued sides, 0.8 cm from the edge, then use the bradawl to double the size of the holes.

4. Sew along these lines with the orange thread, using saddle stitch (see page 64).

5. Glue two of the leather strips together along their entire surface, wrong sides facing. Hold them in place with clothes pegs. Repeat this process with the other two strips and leave both handles to dry.

6. Use the rotary punch to mark out a square measuring 1.5 × 1.5 cm at the ends of each handle. Enlarge the holes with the bradawl. Punch matching holes on the top edge of the bag, 7 cm from each side.

7. Sew on the handles by hand with the orange thread, using saddle stitch.

BASIC STITCHES
& MOTIFS

BASIC EMBROIDERY STITCHES

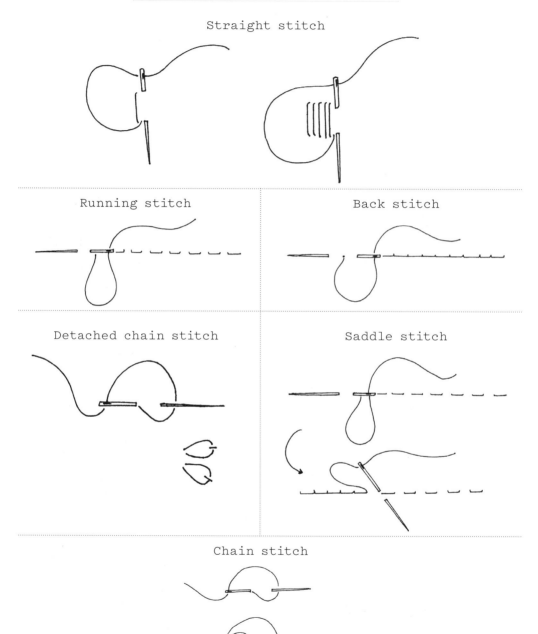

Straight stitch

Running stitch

Back stitch

Detached chain stitch

Saddle stitch

Chain stitch

THIS IS NOT

louis vuitton

not hermès

NOT a billy

jeromeDREYFUSS

EVEN NOT

donop,

be happy

OR

DIE

(0 1 2

3 4 5 6

7 8 9)

0 1 2
3 4 5
6 7 8
9

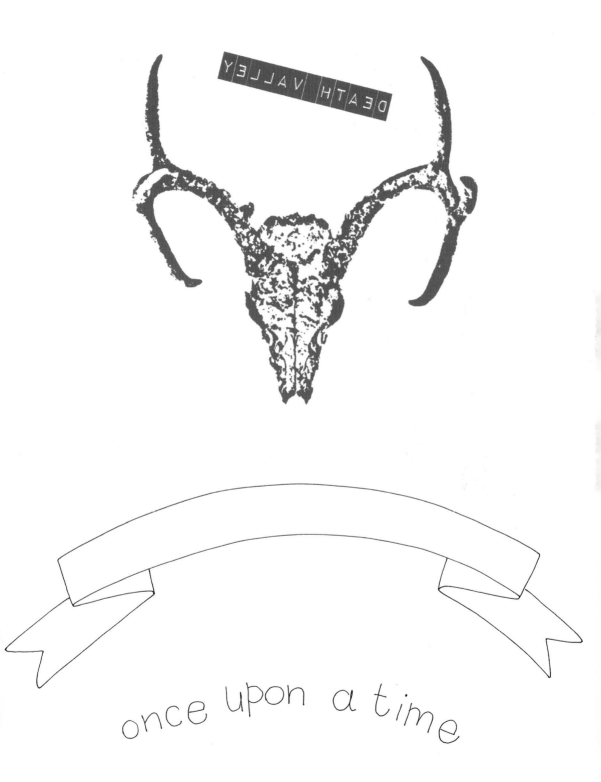

once upon a time

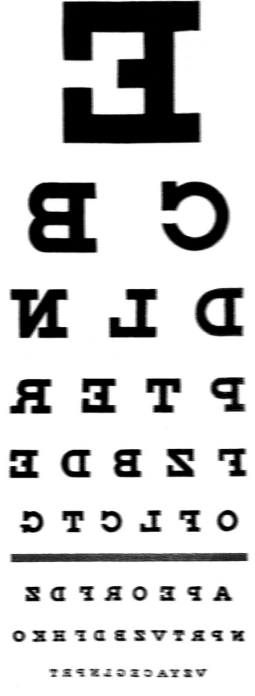

#ilovemytotebag

———— : Chain stitch

– – – : Running stich

 : Detached chain stitch

SEWING TERMS FOR BEGINNERS

HEM

A hem is the stitched edge of a piece of fabric. It is made by folding the fabric in on itself and sewing it down.

OVERSEWING (OR WHIPSTITCHING)

This involves making a series of small stitches passing over the edge of a piece of fabric to prevent it from fraying.

RIGHT SIDES FACING

This term means that when two pieces of fabric are put on top of each other to be sewn together, the printed side of one faces the printed side of the other. After being sewn, the fabric is turned the right way out, so that the stitches are out of sight, on the wrong side.

SEAM ALLOWANCE

Every piece of fabric that is sewn to another has a small border or seam allowance, usually 0.5 cm or 1 cm wide, added to its measurement to allow space for the stitching. The allowance is the distance between the stitches and the edge of the fabric.